2017 SQA Past Papers with Answers

National 5
SPANISH

FREE audio files to accompany this title can be accessed at **www.hoddereducation.co.uk/sqaaudiofiles** You will find the files listed by language and level.

2015, 2016 & 2017 Exams

Hodder Gibson Study Skills Advice – National 5 Spanish	– page 3
Hodder Gibson Study Skills Advice – General	– page 5
2015 EXAM	– page 7
2016 EXAM	– page 37
2017 EXAM	– page 69
ANSWERS	– page 99

HODDER GIBSON
AN HACHETTE UK COMPANY

This book contains the official SQA 2015, 2016 and 2017 Exams for National 5 Spanish, with associated SQA-approved answers modified from the official marking instructions that accompany the paper.

In addition the book contains study skills advice. This has been specially commissioned by Hodder Gibson, and has been written by experienced senior teachers and examiners in line with the new National 5 syllabus and assessment outlines. This is not SQA material but has been devised to provide further guidance for National 5 examinations.

Hodder Gibson is grateful to the copyright holders, as credited on the final page of the Answer section, for permission to use their material. Every effort has been made to trace the copyright holders and to obtain their permission for the use of copyright material. Hodder Gibson will be happy to receive information allowing us to rectify any error or omission in future editions.

Hachette UK's policy is to use papers that are natural, renewable and recyclable products and made from wood grown in sustainable forests. The logging and manufacturing processes are expected to conform to the environmental regulations of the country of origin.

Orders: please contact Bookpoint Ltd, 130 Park Drive, Milton Park, Abingdon, Oxon OX14 4SE. Telephone: (44) 01235 827720. Fax: (44) 01235 400454. Lines are open 9.00–5.00, Monday to Saturday, with a 24-hour message answering service. Visit our website at www.hoddereducation.co.uk. Hodder Gibson can be contacted direct on: Tel: 0141 333 4650; Fax: 0141 404 8188; email: hoddergibson@hodder.co.uk

This collection first published in 2017 by
Hodder Gibson, an imprint of Hodder Education,
An Hachette UK Company
211 St Vincent Street
Glasgow G2 5QY

National 5 2015, 2016 and 2017 Exam Papers and Answers © Scottish Qualifications Authority. Study Skills section © Hodder Gibson. All rights reserved. Apart from any use permitted under UK copyright law, no part of this publication may be reproduced or transmitted in any form or by any means, electronic or mechanical, including photocopying and recording, or held within any information storage and retrieval system, without permission in writing from the publisher or under licence from the Copyright Licensing Agency Limited. Further details of such licences (for reprographic reproduction) may be obtained from the Copyright Licensing Agency Limited, www.cla.co.uk

Typeset by Aptara, Inc.

Printed in the UK

A catalogue record for this title is available from the British Library

ISBN: 978-1-5104-2199-8

2 1

2018 2017

Introduction

National 5 Spanish

The course specifications for National 5 Spanish have changed, and Units and Unit Assessments have been removed. The only change to the exam papers, however, is the removal of "overall purpose" questions for Reading and Listening. The Past Papers have been altered to reflect this, so these remain current and incredibly useful tools for your revision. The questions contained in this book of Past Papers provide excellent representative exam practice. Using them as part of your revision will help you to learn the vital skills and techniques needed for the exam, and will help you to identify any knowledge gaps you may have, prior to the exam season in May–June.

The course

The National 5 Spanish course aims to enable you to develop the ability to read, listen, talk and write in Spanish, that is to understand and use Spanish, and to apply your knowledge and understanding of the language. The course offers the opportunity to develop detailed language skills in the real-life contexts of society, learning, employability, and culture.

How the course is graded

The course assessment will take the form of a performance, a writing assignment and a written exam.

- The performance will be a presentation and discussion with your teacher, which will be recorded and marked by your teacher. It is worth 25% of your final mark.
- The topic for the writing assignment will be agreed between you and your teacher. It will be carried out in class, under supervised conditions. It is worth 12.5% of your final mark.
- The written exam will take place in May and this book will help you practise for it.

The exams

Reading and Writing

- Exam time: 1 hour 30 minutes
- Total marks: 50
- Weighting in final grade: 37.5%

What you have to do

- Read three passages of just under 200 words each, and answer questions about them in English.
- Write 120–200 words in Spanish in the form of an email, applying for a job or work placement: there will be six bullet points for you to address.

Listening

- Exam time: 25 minutes
- Total marks: 20
- Weighting in final grade: 25%

What you have to do

- Part 1: listen to a presentation in Spanish, and answer questions in English.
- Part 2: listen to a conversation in Spanish, and answer questions about it in English.

How to improve your mark!

Every year, examiners notice the same kind of mistakes being made, and they also regularly come across some excellent work. They give advice in the three key areas of reading, listening and writing to help students do better. Here are some key points from their advice.

Reading

Make sure that your Reading answers include detail. Remember, an answer of only one word will not normally be enough to gain a mark. However, you do not have to answer in full sentences; bullet points are fine. Use each question as a guide to where to look, and what to look for. In the question there will be a clear guide to the context for the answer. Detailed answers are generally required, so pay particular attention to words like "más", "siempre", "bastante", etc. and to negatives. "Los sábados por la tarde" isn't just Saturday, and "a principios del mes de agosto" isn't just August, so be prepared to give all the details you can find.

Make sure you get the details of numbers, days, times etc. right.

Take care when using a dictionary when a word has more than one meaning. Learn to choose the correct meaning from a list of meanings in the dictionary.

Beware of false friends: "compartir" means share, not compare, and "esta de buen humor" does not mean he has a sense of humour, rather he is in a good mood.

In responding to the questions in the Reading papers, you should be guided by the number of points awarded for each question. You should give as much detail in your answer as you have understood, but you should not put down everything which is in the original text, as you would be wasting time. The question itself usually indicates the amount of information required by stating in bold, e.g. "State **two** things" or "Give **any two** reasons". If the question says "state any two things" it means there are more than two possibilities. Just choose the two you are happiest with and stick to them. Only give alternatives if you are absolutely unsure of what is correct.

If you have time at the end, you should re-read your answers to make sure that they make sense and that your English expression is as good as it can be.

Listening

This is the paper that improves most with practice. So use the Listening papers in this book several times to get used to the format of the exam.

Not giving enough detail is still a major reason for candidates losing marks. Many answers are correct as far as they go, but are not sufficiently detailed to score marks. The rules for Reading also apply here.

You hear each of the Listening texts three times, so make use of the third listening to check the accuracy and specific details of your answers.

Be sure you are able to give accurate answers through confident knowledge of numbers, common adjectives, weather expressions, prepositions and question words, so that some of the "easier" points of information are not lost through lack of sufficiently accurate details.

In responding to the questions in the Listening papers, you should be guided by the number of points awarded for each question, and by the wording of the question. You should give as much detail in your answer as you have understood, but you should not write down everything you hear. The question itself usually indicates the amount of information required by stating in bold, e.g. "**State two of them**".

Make sure you put a line through any notes you have made.

Writing

This, along with Talking, is often where students do best. It is a chance for you to know what your answers to the first four bullet points are in advance. Make sure you have some good material prepared and learned, ready to use in the exam.

Also, where learners write pieces that are too lengthy, this certainly does not help their performance. So stick to 20–30 words per bullet point.

On the whole, the majority of candidates write well, and the range of language used is impressive. So look at the success criteria in the answer section and try to model your writing on it. This applies particularly to the last two bullet points. Practise writing answers to the final two bullet points, which are different in every exam, adapting material you already know rather than using a dictionary to translate ideas from English.

You should ensure that you are careful when you read the information regarding the job you are applying for, and make sure your answer is tailored to fit that. Depending on the job, you may have to alter your strengths or the experience you are claiming. You should prepare in Spanish a description of some "soft" skills that are transferable, for instance, working with the public, able to communicate, good at working as part of a team or with others. Use your dictionary to make sure you know what the job actually is, if necessary.

Use the dictionary to check the accuracy of what you have written (spelling, accents, genders, etc.) but not to create new sentences, particularly when dealing with the last two bullet points. You should have everything you need prepared when you come into the exam.

Be aware of the extended criteria to be used in assessing performances in Writing, so that you know what is required in terms of content, accuracy, range and variety of language to achieve the "good" and "very good" categories. Ensure that your handwriting is legible (particularly when writing in Spanish) and distinguish clearly between rough notes and what you wish to be considered as final answers. Make sure you score out your notes!

You should bear the following points in mind:

- There are six bullet points to answer: the first four are always the same, the last two vary from year to year.
- Each of the first four bullet points should have between 25 and 30 words to address it properly.
- Answering the first four bullet points correctly will get you 12/20. Each of the last two, if answered correctly, will get an additional 4 marks.
- You should aim to write about 20 words for each of these last two points, but do not try to write too much, as this might mean you are more likely to get things wrong.
- You will be assessed on how well you have answered the points, and on the accuracy of your language.
- You should also try to have a variety of tenses in your preparation for the first four bullet points, including past, future and conditional if you can.
- For a mark of "good" or "very good", you should have some complex language, such as longer, varied sentences and conjunctions. So, have some sub-clauses ready, starting with words like "y", "o", "pero", "porque", "cuando", etc.

Good luck!

Remember that the rewards for passing National 5 Spanish are well worth it! Your pass will help you get the future you want for yourself. In the exam, be confident in your own ability. If you're not sure how to answer a question, trust your instincts and give it a go anyway – keep calm and don't panic! GOOD LUCK!

Study Skills – what you need to know to pass exams!

Pause for thought

Many students might skip quickly through a page like this. After all, we all know how to revise. Do you really though?

Think about this:

"IF YOU ALWAYS DO WHAT YOU ALWAYS DO, YOU WILL ALWAYS GET WHAT YOU HAVE ALWAYS GOT."

Do you like the grades you get? Do you want to do better? If you get full marks in your assessment, then that's great! Change nothing! This section is just to help you get that little bit better than you already are.

There are two main parts to the advice on offer here. The first part highlights fairly obvious things but which are also very important. The second part makes suggestions about revision that you might not have thought about but which WILL help you.

Part 1

DOH! It's so obvious but …

Start revising in good time

Don't leave it until the last minute – this will make you panic.

Make a revision timetable that sets out work time AND play time.

Sleep and eat!

Obvious really, and very helpful. Avoid arguments or stressful things too – even games that wind you up. You need to be fit, awake and focused!

Know your place!

Make sure you know exactly **WHEN and WHERE** your exams are.

Know your enemy!

Make sure you know what to expect in the exam.

How is the paper structured?

How much time is there for each question?

What types of question are involved?

Which topics seem to come up time and time again?

Which topics are your strongest and which are your weakest?

Are all topics compulsory or are there choices?

Learn by DOING!

There is no substitute for past papers and practice papers – they are simply essential! Tackling this collection of papers and answers is exactly the right thing to be doing as your exams approach.

Part 2

People learn in different ways. Some like low light, some bright. Some like early morning, some like evening / night. Some prefer warm, some prefer cold. But everyone uses their BRAIN and the brain works when it is active. Passive learning – sitting gazing at notes – is the most INEFFICIENT way to learn anything. Below you will find tips and ideas for making your revision more effective and maybe even more enjoyable. What follows gets your brain active, and active learning works!

Activity 1 – Stop and review

Step 1

When you have done no more than 5 minutes of revision reading STOP!

Step 2

Write a heading in your own words which sums up the topic you have been revising.

Step 3

Write a summary of what you have revised in no more than two sentences. Don't fool yourself by saying, "I know it, but I cannot put it into words". That just means you don't know it well enough. If you cannot write your summary, revise that section again, knowing that you must write a summary at the end of it. Many of you will have notebooks full of blue/black ink writing. Many of the pages will not be especially attractive or memorable so try to liven them up a bit with colour as you are reviewing and rewriting. **This is a great memory aid, and memory is the most important thing.**

Activity 2 – Use technology!

Why should everything be written down? Have you thought about "mental" maps, diagrams, cartoons and colour to help you learn? And rather than write down notes, why not record your revision material?

What about having a text message revision session with friends? Keep in touch with them to find out how and what they are revising and share ideas and questions.

Why not make a video diary where you tell the camera what you are doing, what you think you have learned and what you still have to do? No one has to see or hear it, but the process of having to organise your thoughts in a formal way to explain something is a very important learning practice.

Be sure to make use of electronic files. You could begin to summarise your class notes. Your typing might be slow, but it will get faster and the typed notes will be easier to read than the scribbles in your class notes. Try to add different fonts and colours to make your work stand out. You can easily Google relevant pictures, cartoons and diagrams which you can copy and paste to make your work more attractive and **MEMORABLE**.

Activity 3 – This is it. Do this and you will know lots!

Step 1

In this task you must be very honest with yourself! Find the SQA syllabus for your subject (www.sqa.org.uk). Look at how it is broken down into main topics called MANDATORY knowledge. That means stuff you MUST know.

Step 2

BEFORE you do ANY revision on this topic, write a list of everything that you already know about the subject. It might be quite a long list but you only need to write it once. It shows you all the information that is already in your long-term memory so you know what parts you do not need to revise!

Step 3

Pick a chapter or section from your book or revision notes. Choose a fairly large section or a whole chapter to get the most out of this activity.

With a buddy, use Skype, Facetime, Twitter or any other communication you have, to play the game "If this is the answer, what is the question?". For example, if you are revising Geography and the answer you provide is "meander", your buddy would have to make up a question like "What is the word that describes a feature of a river where it flows slowly and bends often from side to side?".

Make up 10 "answers" based on the content of the chapter or section you are using. Give this to your buddy to solve while you solve theirs.

Step 4

Construct a wordsearch of at least 10 × 10 squares. You can make it as big as you like but keep it realistic. Work together with a group of friends. Many apps allow you to make wordsearch puzzles online. The words and phrases can go in any direction and phrases can be split. Your puzzle must only contain facts linked to the topic you are revising. Your task is to find 10 bits of information to hide in your puzzle, but you must not repeat information that you used in Step 3. DO NOT show where the words are. Fill up empty squares with random letters. Remember to keep a note of where your answers are hidden but do not show your friends. When you have a complete puzzle, exchange it with a friend to solve each other's puzzle.

Step 5

Now make up 10 questions (not "answers" this time) based on the same chapter used in the previous two tasks. Again, you must find NEW information that you have not yet used. Now it's getting hard to find that new information! Again, give your questions to a friend to answer.

Step 6

As you have been doing the puzzles, your brain has been actively searching for new information. Now write a NEW LIST that contains only the new information you have discovered when doing the puzzles. Your new list is the one to look at repeatedly for short bursts over the next few days. Try to remember more and more of it without looking at it. After a few days, you should be able to add words from your second list to your first list as you increase the information in your long-term memory.

FINALLY! Be inspired...

Make a list of different revision ideas and beside each one write **THINGS I HAVE** tried, **THINGS I WILL** try and **THINGS I MIGHT** try. Don't be scared of trying something new.

And remember – "FAIL TO PREPARE AND PREPARE TO FAIL!"

NATIONAL 5
2015

FOR OFFICIAL USE

N5 National Qualifications 2015

Mark

X769/75/01

Spanish Reading

FRIDAY, 29 MAY
9:00 AM – 10:30 AM

Fill in these boxes and read what is printed below.

Full name of centre: Stewarts Melville College

Town: Edinburgh

Forename(s): Lewis Alexander

Surname: Dundas

Number of seat:

Date of birth
Day: 3 1   Month: 1 0   Year: 0 3

Scottish candidate number: 0 2 0 5 9 6 7 7 2

Total marks — 30

Attempt ALL questions.

Write your answers clearly, in **English**, in the spaces provided in this booklet.

You may use a Spanish dictionary.

Additional space for answers is provided at the end of this booklet. If you use this space you must clearly identify the question number you are attempting.

Use **blue** or **black** ink.

There is a separate question and answer booklet for Writing. You must complete your answer for Writing in the question and answer booklet for Writing.

Before leaving the examination room you must give both booklets to the Invigilator; if you do not, you may lose all the marks for this paper.

Total marks — 30

Attempt ALL questions

Text 1

You read an article about young people and part-time jobs.

TRABAJAR Y ESTUDIAR CON 16 AÑOS

Como joven es probable que tengas algún tiempo libre y el deseo de ganar dinero. Además de ofrecerte una fuente de ingresos para tus gastos personales, el primer empleo te permitirá independizarte, y ver cómo funciona el mundo de los negocios.

Un poco de dinero extra siempre viene bien para salir de juerga con los amigos y para ahorrar para el carné de conducir. Sin embargo, compaginar estudios y trabajo es un desafío para muchos que no tienen tiempo de terminar todos los deberes del instituto. Los trabajos típicos incluyen rellenar estantes en el supermercado, repartir periódicos en el barrio o cuidar niños de los parientes.

Natalia Méndez Goya, de dieciséis años, dice: «*Pues yo gano dinero extra enseñando a mi abuelo de setenta y tres años a utilizar internet y antes de ir al colegio paseo los dos perros de mi vecino.*»

Se recomienda que los jóvenes no trabajen de noche durante la semana porque les resultará muy difícil levantarse temprano por la mañana para llegar al instituto a tiempo. Entre los jóvenes que trabajan por la noche, muchos van a clase dormidos o sin haber tenido tiempo de desayunar y por lo tanto no aprenden prácticamente nada.

Questions

(a) Complete the following sentence.

As a young person you will probably have some free time and _____

_____.

(b) What will your first job allow you to do? State any **one** thing.

_____

Text 1 Questions (continued)

(c) How can you spend extra money? State **two** things. [2]

(d) What jobs do young people typically do? Give details of any **two**. [2]

(e) Natalia Méndez Goya talks about her part-time jobs. What does she do to earn extra money? State any **one** thing. [1]

(f) (i) Why should young people not work at night? [1]

    (ii) What can happen to many young people who do work at night? State any **one** thing. [1]

(g) What does the article say about part-time jobs? Tick (✓) the correct box. [1]

Having a part-time job while studying is something all young people should do.	
Having a part-time job while studying is difficult for many young people.	
Having a part-time job and studying is very popular in Spain.	

[Turn over

Text 2

You read an article about a museum in Madrid.

El Museo de Arte Moderno

El Museo de Arte Moderno en Madrid va a celebrar su quinto aniversario con unas jornadas de puertas abiertas. Se podrán visitar, con acceso gratuito, las nuevas esculturas norteamericanas. Además, se ha creado una exposición de arte moderno europeo.

Dolores Rodríguez, directora del museo, informa: "estamos seguros de que ofrecemos una gran selección de arte que a todos los visitantes les va a apasionar. Al visitar el museo, la gente puede descubrir a artistas menos conocidos además de mirar pinturas de los últimos cincuenta años."

El público también tendrá la oportunidad de participar en la celebración votando por su obra de arte favorita. Pueden dar su opinión a través de las pantallas táctiles en las salas del museo o rellenando una encuesta en la página web.

El horario será el habitual de lunes a sábado, de diez a siete horas de la tarde. Si las jornadas tienen mucho éxito, Dolores tiene planes de organizar más días de acceso gratuito para los jubilados.

Questions

(a) Which anniversary is the museum celebrating? **1**

(b) The museum is having a series of open days. What will people be able to visit? State **two** things. **2**

Text 2 Questions (continued)

(c) Dolores Rodríguez says the museum offers a large selection of art. According to Dolores, what will visitors think of it? **1**

(d) What can people do during their visit? Complete the sentence. **2**

People can discover _____ and

they can look at paintings _____ .

(e) The public is encouraged to participate in the museum's anniversary.

   (i) How can they take part in the celebration? **1**

   (ii) How will they be able to give their opinion? State **two** things. **2**

(f) What plans does Dolores have for the museum? **1**

[Turn over

Text 3

You read an article about facial recognition software which is being developed for use in cars.

El reconocimiento facial dentro del coche

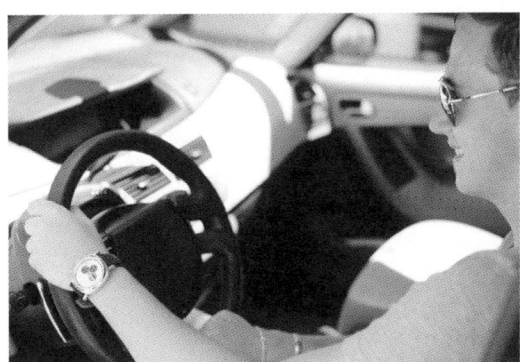

La mayor parte de los accidentes de tráfico son debidos al conductor, por ejemplo si el conductor conduce con un exceso de velocidad o sin prudencia. Así que no es de extrañar que cada vez más fabricantes de automóviles trabajen en el desarrollo de una tecnología que emplea una cámara de vídeo y un *software* de reconocimiento facial para intentar mejorar la seguridad durante la conducción.

La cámara grabará los cambios de las expresiones faciales, movimientos musculares, y emociones del rostro del conductor. Además, el sistema tendrá que estar permanentemente vigilante para poder reconocer si el conductor está distraído, si está sufriendo somnolencia o si no está en condiciones de seguir conduciendo.

Hay alguna dificultad. Hay que buscar la mejor posición para la cámara para que tenga una buena visión del rostro del conductor.

Este sistema puede advertir al conductor de que no está en condiciones para conducir por hacer sonar una alarma cinco veces si está durmiendo.

No cabe duda alguna de que reducir los riesgos al factor humano de una manera tecnológica es positivo. Por ejemplo, puede ayudar al conductor a actuar para evitar un accidente.

Questions

(a) Complete the following sentence.

Most traffic accidents are the fault of the driver. For example if the driver is driving _____ or _____ .

Text 3 Questions (continued)

(b) What is the purpose of facial recognition software in cars? **1**

(c) What will the camera record? State any **two** things. **2**

(d) Why will the system have to be permanently switched on? State any **two** things. **2**

(e) How can the system warn drivers? Give **two** details. **2**

(f) According to the final paragraph, why is this type of technology positive? **1**

[END OF QUESTION PAPER]

ADDITIONAL SPACE FOR ANSWERS

ADDITIONAL SPACE FOR ANSWERS

N5

National Qualifications 2015

FOR OFFICIAL USE

Mark

X769/75/02

Spanish Writing

FRIDAY, 29 MAY
9:00 AM – 10:30 AM

Fill in these boxes and read what is printed below.

Full name of centre

Town

Forename(s)

Surname

Number of seat

Date of birth
Day   Month   Year

Scottish candidate number

Total marks — 20

Write your answer clearly, in **Spanish**, in the space provided in this booklet.

You may use a Spanish dictionary.

Additional space for answers is provided at the end of this booklet.

Use **blue** or **black** ink.

There is a separate question and answer booklet for Reading. You must complete your answers for Reading in the question and answer booklet for Reading.

Before leaving the examination room you must give both booklets to the Invigilator; if you do not, you may lose all the marks for this paper.

Total marks — 20

You are preparing an application for the job advertised below and you write an e-mail in **Spanish** to the company.

Se necesita dependiente/dependienta

Se requiere una persona seria, dinámica y responsable para trabajar en una tienda de ropa en Sevilla.

Imprescindible hablar inglés y preferiblemente otro idioma. Buena presencia esencial.

Se ruega escribir al director de la tienda:
manuel.garciaramirez@tiendaroja.es

To help you to write your e-mail, you have been given the following checklist.

You must include **all** of these points:

- Personal details (name, age, where you live)
- School/college/education experience until now
- Skills/interests you have which make you right for the job
- Related work experience
- Languages spoken
- Reasons for application

Use all of the above to help you write the e-mail in **Spanish**. The e-mail should be approximately 120–150 words. You may use a Spanish dictionary.

ANSWER SPACE

[Turn over

ANSWER SPACE (continued)

ANSWER SPACE (continued)

ANSWER SPACE (continued)

[END OF QUESTION PAPER]

…

ADDITIONAL SPACE FOR ANSWERS

FOR OFFICIAL USE

N5 National Qualifications 2015

Mark

X769/75/03

Spanish Listening

FRIDAY, 29 MAY
10:50 AM – 11:15 AM (approx)

Fill in these boxes and read what is printed below.

Full name of centre

Town

Forename(s)

Surname

Number of seat

Date of birth
Day   Month   Year

Scottish candidate number

Total marks — 20

Attempt ALL questions.

You will hear two items in Spanish. **Before you hear each item, you will have one minute to study the questions.** You will hear each item three times, with an interval of one minute between playings. You will then have time to answer the questions before hearing the next item.

You may NOT use a Spanish dictionary.

Write your answers clearly, in **English**, in the spaces provided in this booklet. Additional space for answers is provided at the end of this booklet. If you use this space you must clearly identify the question number you are attempting.

Use **blue** or **black** ink.

You are not allowed to leave the examination room until the end of the test.

Before leaving the examination room you must give this booklet to the Invigilator; if you do not, you may lose all the marks for this paper.

Total marks — 20

Attempt ALL questions

Item 1

Luisa talks about languages.

(a) What does Luisa say about her mum? State any **one** thing. **1**

(b) What makes Luisa's English classes fun? State any **one** thing. **1**

(c) Apart from computers, what other kind of technology does she use in her English class? **1**

(d) Luisa talks about the advantage of speaking different languages. What does she say? **1**

(e) Luisa went to a summer camp last year. Where did she go? **1**

(f) What does she want to do when she finishes her studies? State **two** things. **2**

(g) Which statement best matches Luisa's attitude to languages? Tick (✓) the correct statement. **1**

She really likes them but they are just another school subject.	
She thinks they are good for holidays.	
They play an important part in many areas of her life.	

Item 2

Francisco talks to Luisa about his exams.

(a) How much time does Francisco spend revising? **1**

_____

(b) He gives details of the exam timetable. Tick (✓) the **two** correct statements. **2**

The exams start the next day.	
The first exam is Biology.	
The exams finish on the 12th of June.	
They last for 17 days in total.	

(c) Why does he prefer studying with a friend? State any **two** things. **2**

_____

_____

(d) How does he relax when he has a break? State any **two** things. **2**

_____

_____

(e) What does he find difficult about History? **1**

_____

(f) Francisco says the weather is nice. What would he rather be doing? State any **two** things. **2**

_____

_____

(g) Francisco is anxious about his Maths exam. Why? State any **two** things. **2**

_____

_____

[END OF QUESTION PAPER]

ADDITIONAL SPACE FOR ANSWERS

ADDITIONAL SPACE FOR ANSWERS

National Qualifications 2015

X769/75/13

**Spanish
Listening Transcript**

FRIDAY, 29 MAY

10:50 AM – 11:15 AM (approx)

This paper must not be seen by any candidate.

The material overleaf is provided for use in an emergency only (eg the recording or equipment proving faulty) or where permission has been given in advance by SQA for the material to be read to candidates with additional support needs. The material must be read exactly as printed.

Instructions to reader(s)

For each item, read the English **once**, then read the Spanish **three times**, with an interval of 1 minute between the three readings. On completion of the third reading, pause for the length of time indicated in brackets after the item, to allow the candidates to write their answers.

Where special arrangements have been agreed in advance to allow the reading of the material, those sections marked **(f)** should be read by a female speaker and those marked **(m)** by a male; those sections marked **(t)** should be read by the teacher.

(t)   Item Number One

Luisa talks about languages.

You now have one minute to study the questions for Item Number One.

(f)   Siempre me han interesado los idiomas. Creo que es porque mi madre es suiza y habla muchas lenguas . . . francés, italiano y alemán.

Además, este año tengo suerte porque en el colegio tenemos una profesora de inglés que es muy entusiasta. Sus clases son muy divertidas – aprendemos canciones y ella tiene muy buen sentido del humor. También, utilizo la tecnología a menudo, es decir los ordenadores y la pizarra interactiva así que las clases son muy interesantes. Una ventaja de aprender lenguas es que puedo ayudar a muchos de los turistas extranjeros que visitan mi ciudad cada año.

El año pasado pasé un mes en un campamento de verano en la costa este de Irlanda – me lo pasé de maravilla y mi inglés ha mejorado mucho.

He decidido que cuando termine mis estudios quisiera encontrar trabajo en una empresa internacional y viajar por todo el mundo.

Lo tengo muy claro, todos los jóvenes deberían hablar una lengua además de la materna.

(2 minutes)

(t) Item Number Two

Francisco talks to Luisa about his exams.

You now have one minute to study the questions for Item Number Two.

(f) Hace mucho que no te veo, Francisco . . . ¿qué tal?

(m) En este momento estoy preparando mis exámenes de fin de curso. Cada tarde paso tres horas repasando mis asignaturas.

(f) Y ¿cuándo son estos exámenes?

(m) Empiezan el martes por la mañana . . . el primero es biología. Terminan el 11 de junio con informática. Así que en total duran 17 días. ¡Qué tostón!

(f) No es fácil trabajar solo ¿verdad?

(m) Tienes razón, pero a veces mi amigo Vicente viene a mi casa y trabajamos juntos, creo que aprendo mejor, el tiempo pasa más rápido y no me aburro tanto.

(f) Pero es importante también tomarse un descanso de vez en cuando ¿no?

(m) Sí, sí . . . me tomo un descanso cada hora para comer unas galletas, llamar a mis amigos o mirar una telenovela durante diez minutos . . . depende.

(f) Y estudiar ¿te parece fácil?

(m) Para mí lo más difícil es la historia, me cuesta mucho memorizar las fechas importantes.

(f) Sí . . . pero creo que es igual para todo el mundo.

(m) Lo peor es que en este momento hace buen tiempo y me gustaría estar al aire libre para dar una vuelta en bici o entrenarme con mi club de natación. Pero no hay más remedio.

(f) Bueno, por lo menos pareces muy relajado.

(m) ¡No! El miércoles tengo exámen de matemáticas. Estoy un poco preocupado porque creo que no he trabajado bastante en clase. Además, no me siento muy bien y me duele un poco la garganta. ¡Ojalá que todo salga bien!

(2 minutes)

(t) End of test.

Now look over your answers.

[END OF TRANSCRIPT]

NATIONAL 5

2016

SQA

HODDER GIBSON
LEARN MORE

N5 National Qualifications 2016

X769/75/01

Spanish Reading

THURSDAY, 26 MAY
1:00 PM – 2:30 PM

Fill in these boxes and read what is printed below.

Full name of centre

Town

Forename(s)

Surname

Number of seat

Date of birth
Day Month Year

Scottish candidate number

Total marks — 30

Attempt ALL questions.

Write your answers clearly, in **English**, in the spaces provided in this booklet.

You may use a Spanish dictionary.

Additional space for answers is provided at the end of this booklet. If you use this space you must clearly identify the question number you are attempting.

Use **blue** or **black** ink.

There is a separate question and answer booklet for Writing. You must complete your answer for Writing in the question and answer booklet for Writing.

Before leaving the examination room you must give both booklets to the Invigilator; if you do not, you may lose all the marks for this paper.

SQA

Total marks — 30

Attempt ALL questions

Text 1

You read an article about a beach clean-up.

Cuarenta voluntarios para limpiar la playa

Unos cuarenta voluntarios trabajaron ayer para limpiar la playa de Sant Antoni en Ibiza. Los voluntarios al final de la jornada llenaron más de cincuenta bolsas con basura. El grupo, formado tanto por personas jóvenes como por familias, se reunió sobre las diez de la mañana en la playa.

Para algunos, como Carlos Aguado, era la primera vez que participaban. Carlos decidió participar en el voluntariado al ver el daño que ha sufrido la costa estos últimos años. Después de la limpieza, Carlos comentaba que "Lo que más he encontrado son colillas, vidrio roto y bolsas de supermercado".

La jornada de limpieza también contó con el apoyo de los turistas. Una pareja británica, tras enterarse de esta campaña, decidió ayudar: "Queremos proteger la belleza de la playa."

El objetivo de esta limpieza es concienciar a la gente sobre la importancia de no tirar los residuos al mar. "No esperábamos a tanta gente", explicó Eva Marqués, organizadora. "En mi opinión, creo que el medio ambiente interesa a mucha gente", añadió. Después de este éxito, es seguro que en el futuro Eva organizará jornadas de limpieza en los parques y visitas escolares para informar a los alumnos.

Questions

(a) (i) How much rubbish did the volunteers collect from the beach? 1

Text 1 Questions (continued)

(ii) At what time did the group meet?

(b) For Carlos Aguado, it was his first time cleaning up the beach.

(i) What did Carlos see that made him decide to participate?

(ii) What sort of rubbish does he say he found? Give details of any **two** things.

(c) Some tourists also took part in the clean-up. Why did a British couple decide to help? Give details.

(d) Complete the sentence.

The purpose of this beach clean-up is to make people aware of the importance of not _____.

(e) Eva Marqués organised the clean-up.

(i) Why does Eva think that so many people turned up?

(ii) What will she organise in the future? State **two** things.

Text 2

You read an article about International Girls' Day.

El Día Internacional de la Niña

Según una organización internacional, muchas niñas en varios paises del mundo hacen frente al problema de la falta de educación. Las Naciones Unidas han declarado el 11 de octubre como Día Internacional de la Niña.

El objetivo del Día Internacional de la Niña es de reconocer los derechos de las niñas, de intentar solucionar los problemas excepcionales que enfrentan las niñas, y de aumentar la proporción de niñas que completan la educación básica.

75 millones de niñas no van al colegio

Un estudio reciente demuestra que un tercio de niñas en el mundo no completa la educación secundaria y el 24 por ciento de las mujeres son analfabetas.

Muchas niñas se incorporan a la fuerza laboral a una edad temprana y suelen hacer los trabajos peor remunerados y menos valorados, por ejemplo en el servicio doméstico.

Un futuro optimista en El Salvador

Con el apoyo internacional, la vida de más de 5000 niñas de El Salvador ha mejorado muchísimo porque han podido estudiar un año más. Como resultado tienen la posibilidad de acceder a mejores empleos y de generar más ingresos para sus familias.

Questions

(a) According to an international organisation, what problem do many girls face?
1

(b) What is the aim of International Girls' Day? State any **two** things.
2

(c) Complete the sentence.
2

According to a recent study, a third of girls in the world _____

and 24% of women are _____ .

(d) Many girls join the work force at an early age. What types of jobs do girls often do? State any **two**.
2

(e) In what **three** ways have the lives of more than 5000 girls in El Salvador improved?
3

[Turn over

Text 3

You read an article about the increase in people working from home.

Trabajar desde casa

Cada vez son más los empleados que "teletrabajan", o sea, que trabajan en casa. Este método de trabajar desde fuera de la oficina es aún más popular en España impulsado por mejor acceso a Internet y las tecnologías de la comunicación.

Además de reportar beneficios económicos, puede aumentar la productividad para las empresas. Y, para los trabajadores, trabajar a distancia permite que se pueda equilibrar la vida laboral con la vida familiar.

Elena Torres es técnico de recursos humanos. Lleva más de tres años teletrabajando para su compañía y está satisfecha con el sistema de teletrabajo. Dice: "Me conecto a Internet para estar comunicada constantemente con mis compañeros. Y puedo hacerlo desde casa o, entre cita y cita, desde un café o un parque."

De lunes a viernes, Elena sigue exactamente la misma rutina diaria: se levanta bastante temprano, toma su desayuno mientras lee su correo electrónico, se viste con ropa cómoda y anda un par de pasos hasta el salón de su casa.

"Gracias al teletrabajo, mi vida ha mejorado mucho. Me organizo el tiempo a mi manera", resume.

Questions

(a) Working at home is becoming more popular in Spain. What **two** reasons does the article give for this?   2

Text 3 Questions (continued)

(b) The article describes the benefits of working from home.

(i) As well as economic benefits, what is the other advantage for companies? **1**

(ii) What is the main benefit for workers? **1**

(c) Elena Torres explains why she is satisfied with this way of working. What does she say? State any **two** things. **2**

(d) She describes her daily routine from Monday to Friday. What does she say? State any **three** things. **3**

(e) What does Elena think about working from home? Tick (✓) the correct statement. **1**

	Tick (✓)
Working from home has made her life more comfortable.	
Working from home can be difficult.	
Working from home has many advantages.	

[END OF QUESTION PAPER]

ADDITIONAL SPACE FOR ANSWERS

ADDITIONAL SPACE FOR ANSWERS

[BLANK PAGE]

DO NOT WRITE ON THIS PAGE

FOR OFFICIAL USE

N5 National Qualifications 2016

Mark

X769/75/02

Spanish Writing

THURSDAY, 26 MAY
1:00 PM – 2:30 PM

Fill in these boxes and read what is printed below.

Full name of centre

Town

Forename(s)

Surname

Number of seat

Date of birth
Day Month Year

Scottish candidate number

Total marks — 20

Write your answer clearly, in **Spanish**, in the space provided in this booklet.

You may use a Spanish dictionary.

Additional space for answers is provided at the end of this booklet.

Use **blue** or **black** ink.

There is a separate question and answer booklet for Reading. You must complete your answers for Reading in the question and answer booklet for Reading.

Before leaving the examination room you must give both booklets to the Invigilator; if you do not, you may lose all the marks for this paper.

SQA

Total marks — 20

You are preparing an application for the job advertised below and you write an e-mail in **Spanish** to the company.

Buscamos camarero/a

La heladería 'El Cucurucho', necesita **camarero/a** con conocimiento perfecto del inglés para este verano.

Las responsabilidades principales serán: preparar y servir los helados caseros en nuestro renombrado salón.

Se requiere una persona trabajadora con excelentes habilidades para la comunicación.

Envía tu currículum a *elcucurucho@heladería.es*

To help you to write your e-mail, you have been given the following checklist.
You must include **all** of these points:

- Personal details (name, age, where you live)
- School/college/education experience until now
- Skills/interests you have which make you right for the job
- Related work experience
- When you are available to work in the summer
- Your future career plans

Use all of the above to help you write the e-mail in **Spanish**. The e-mail should be approximately 120–150 words. You may use a Spanish dictionary.

ANSWER SPACE

ANSWER SPACE (continued)

ANSWER SPACE (continued)

ANSWER SPACE (continued)

[END OF QUESTION PAPER]

ADDITIONAL SPACE FOR ANSWERS

ADDITIONAL SPACE FOR ANSWERS

FOR OFFICIAL USE

N5 National Qualifications 2016

Mark

X769/75/03

Spanish Listening

THURSDAY, 26 MAY
2:50 PM – 3:20 PM (approx)

Fill in these boxes and read what is printed below.

Full name of centre

Town

Forename(s)

Surname

Number of seat

Date of birth
Day   Month   Year

Scottish candidate number

Total marks — 20

Attempt ALL questions.

You will hear two items in Spanish. **Before you hear each item, you will have one minute to study the questions.** You will hear each item three times, with an interval of one minute between playings. You will then have time to answer the questions before hearing the next item.

You may NOT use a Spanish dictionary.

Write your answers clearly, in **English**, in the spaces provided in this booklet. Additional space for answers is provided at the end of this booklet. If you use this space you must clearly identify the question number you are attempting.

Use **blue** or **black** ink.

You are not allowed to leave the examination room until the end of the test.

Before leaving the examination room you must give this booklet to the Invigilator; if you do not, you may lose all the marks for this paper.

SQA

Total marks — 20

Attempt ALL questions

Item 1

Gabriela talks about reading.

(a) Complete the table. 2

When does she read?	For how long?
	Half an hour
Every evening	

(b) When she was a child, who read poems and stories to her? 1

_____

(c) What does she now prefer to read? 1

_____

(d) Why does she not like science fiction novels? State any **one** thing. 1

_____

(e) Gabriela uses her tablet for reading. What else does she use it for? State **two** things. 2

_____

_____

(f) Which statement best describes Gabriela's reason for reading? Tick (✓) the correct statement. 1

	Tick (✓)
She reads to help her with her school work.	
She reads for enjoyment.	
She reads when she is bored.	

Page two

[Turn over for next question

DO NOT WRITE ON THIS PAGE

Item 2

Ana tells Javi about the International Music Festival of Benicàssim.

(a) When did Ana first go to the Benicàssim Festival? **1**

(b) How long does the festival last? **1**

(c) What does Ana like most about the festival? **1**

(d) Apart from the concerts, what else does the festival have to offer? State any **two** things. **2**

(e) There is also a free camping zone at the festival. What can you do there? State **two** things. **2**

(f) Ana talks about where she stayed the last time she went to the festival.

   (i) Why did she not go camping? **1**

   (ii) Where did she stay? Give any **one** detail. **1**

Item 2 (continued)

(g) Why are her parents allowing her to go with her friends this year? Give any **two** reasons. [2]

_____

_____

(h) What is Ana most looking forward to about the festival? Tick (✓) the correct statement. [1]

	Tick (✓)
Staying in the campsite.	
Enjoying the atmosphere.	
Being away without her parents.	
Seeing her favourite band.	

[END OF QUESTION PAPER]

ADDITIONAL SPACE FOR ANSWERS

ADDITIONAL SPACE FOR ANSWERS

N5 National Qualifications 2016

X769/75/13

Spanish
Listening Transcript

THURSDAY, 26 MAY
2:50 PM – 3:20 PM (approx)

This paper must not be seen by any candidate.

The material overleaf is provided for use in an emergency only (eg the recording or equipment proving faulty) or where permission has been given in advance by SQA for the material to be read to candidates with additional support needs. The material must be read exactly as printed.

> **Instructions to reader(s)**
>
> For each item, read the English **once**, then read the Spanish **three times**, with an interval of 1 minute between the three readings. On completion of the third reading, pause for the length of time indicated in brackets after the item, to allow the candidates to write their answers.
>
> Where special arrangements have been agreed in advance to allow the reading of the material, those sections marked **(f)** should be read by a female speaker and those marked **(m)** by a male; those sections marked **(t)** should be read by the teacher.

(t) Item Number One

Gabriela talks about reading.

You now have one minute to study the questions for Item Number One.

(f) Suelo pasar mucho tiempo leyendo, tanto libro en papel como digital. Leo media hora por la mañana cuando me levanto y una hora y media cada tarde. Claro, los fines de semana puedo pasar todo el día leyendo, tumbada en el sofá con mi tablet. Cuando era niña, pasaba mucho tiempo con mi abuelo y él me leía poemas y cuentos infantiles. Ahora, leo de todo pero diría que mi tipo de novela preferida es la novela romántica. Sin embargo, a mí las novelas de ciencia-ficción no me gustan nada — las encuentro un poco aburridas y no son realistas. No entiendo a la gente que no lee nunca. Además de leer en mi tablet, descargo aplicaciones y a veces, compro por Internet. ¡No puedo imaginar la vida sin mi tablet!

(2 minutes)

(t) **Item Number Two**

Ana tells Javi about the International Music Festival of Benicàssim.

You now have one minute to study the questions for Item Number Two.

(m) Oye Ana, ¿tienes planes para el verano?

(f) Bueno, hace dos años fui con mi familia por primera vez al Festival Internacional de Benicàssim y he decidido volver este año.

(m) ¡Qué interesante! ¿Qué tipo de festival es?

(f) Um bueno, es un festival de música que dura cuatro días y ofrece música en directo.

(m) Ah, y ¿qué tipos de música hay?

(f) Hay de todo. Todo tipo de música.

(m) Y ¿qué es lo que más te gusta?

(f) Bueno, lo que más me gusta es que puedo ver artistas y grupos diferentes en el mismo día. Es fenomenal.

(m) Oye pues me gustaría ir. Me parece que no me aburriría nada.

(f) Claro que no. El festival no se limita a ofrecer conciertos. Además, hay cine, teatro, concursos, baile y exposiciones.

(m) Es verdad que hay algo para todo el mundo.

(f) Sí. Incluso hay una zona de acampada gratuita donde se puede descansar y conocer gente de todo el mundo.

(m) Suena estupendo. ¿Tú acampaste?

(f) La última vez, no. Fui con mis padres y no les gusta acampar. Por eso, nos alojamos en la casa de mi tío. Tiene una casa en el centro de un pueblo cercano.

(m) Y este año, ¿vas a ir otra vez con la familia?

(f) Um no. Con la familia, no. Me voy con un grupo de amigos. Mis padres dicen que ahora soy mayor y confían en mí. También soy más independiente. Por eso mis padres me van a dejar ir con mis amigos. ¡Qué bien!

(m) Será fenomenal.

(f) Seguro que sí. Lo que más espero es disfrutar del ambiente. Porque han anunciado unos grupos de maravilla.

(2 minutes)

(t) **End of test.**

Now look over your answers.

[END OF TRANSCRIPT]

N5 National Qualifications 2017

X769/75/01

Spanish Reading

WEDNESDAY, 3 MAY
1:00 PM – 2:30 PM

Fill in these boxes and read what is printed below.

Full name of centre

Town

Forename(s)

Surname

Number of seat

Date of birth
Day Month Year

Scottish candidate number

Total marks — 30

Attempt ALL questions.

Write your answers clearly, in **English**, in the spaces provided in this booklet.

You may use a Spanish dictionary.

Additional space for answers is provided at the end of this booklet. If you use this space you must clearly identify the question number you are attempting.

Use **blue** or **black** ink.

There is a separate question and answer booklet for Writing. You must complete your answer for Writing in the question and answer booklet for Writing.

Before leaving the examination room you must give both booklets to the Invigilator; if you do not, you may lose all the marks for this paper.

Total marks — 30

Attempt ALL questions

Text 1

You read an article about the use of mobile phones in the classroom.

Usar el móvil en clase

Ayer, en una conferencia educativa en Madrid, el experto educativo Juan Rodríguez Sanz describió el móvil como una herramienta muy poderosa en el aula. Hoy en día, existen más de 80.000 *apps* educativas para los móviles inteligentes que tienen muchas ventajas. Son gratuitas y ayudan a aumentar la motivación del alumno.

Muchos profesores insisten en la utilidad del móvil. En los últimos años, se ha creado el puesto de Coordinador Técnico en muchos colegios e institutos. Es un profesor que se encarga del desarrollo de la tecnología en las aulas y tiene que promover todos los usos diferentes de los móviles.

Sin embargo, hay algunos padres que se preocupan. Por ejemplo, Carlota Fuentes Girón cree que su hijo pasa demasiado tiempo con su móvil: "Ir al instituto es el momento ideal para hacer una pausa de la tecnología y relacionarse cara a cara con sus compañeros de clase."

Según el experto Juan Rodríguez Sanz, es lógico usar el móvil en las aulas porque todo el mundo lo usa en su vida cotidiana. Juan cree que en el futuro, la primera frase del profesor, al comienzo de la clase, será "encended los teléfonos móviles" en vez de "abrid los libros".

Questions

(a) Complete the sentence.

Juan Rodríguez Sanz describes mobile phones as _____ _____ in the classroom.

1

(b) According to the article, what are the advantages of educational apps? State **two** things.

2

(c) Many schools now have an IT Coordinator. According to the article, what does this person do? Give **two** details.

2

(d) Carlota Fuentes Girón believes her son spends too much time on his phone in class. What does she think school is the ideal time for? Give details of **two** things.

2

(e) According to Juan Rodríguez Sanz, why is it logical to use mobiles in the classroom? Give details.

1

(f) What does Juan believe a teacher will say at the start of a class in the future? State **two** things.

2

[Turn over

Text 2

You read an article about an online recruitment agency.

Un sitio web de empleo

PrimerPaso es un sitio web de empleo dirigido a estudiantes de dieciséis a veinticinco años. El objetivo de este sitio web es ayudar a los jóvenes a encontrar puestos de trabajo.

Encontrar un trabajo puede ser una tarea difícil porque muchas ofertas de trabajo requieren una licenciatura universitaria y varios años de experiencia laboral. En su sitio web se pueden encontrar ofertas de muchas empresas que buscan a jóvenes para puestos de trabajo a media jornada y de contratos de plazo fijo.

Juan encontró su primer trabajo a través del sitio web *PrimerPaso*. Nos cuenta: "Estaba deseando un trabajo simplemente para costear mi vida diaria. Publiqué mi CV en la web y el día siguiente me enviaron una selección de ofertas de empleo que coincidieron con mi perfil. Estoy contento porque encontré un trabajo que puedo compaginar con mis estudios."

PrimerPaso tiene una sección dedicada a consejos para prepararse para una entrevista. Es crucial enterarse sobre los valores de la empresa y hay que saber exactamente de qué trata el trabajo. Y el sitio web te avisa que no te preocupes si no consigues el puesto dado que encontrarás el trabajo de tus sueños algún día.

Questions

(a) What age group is *PrimerPaso* aimed at? — 1

(b) What do many jobs require? State **two** things. — 2

(c) On the *PrimerPaso* website, you can find job offers from many companies. What do these companies look for? State **two** things. — 2

(d) Juan found his first job through the *PrimerPaso* website.

   (i) Why did he want a job? — 1

   (ii) What happened when he published his CV online? — 1

(e) The website also offers advice about preparing for an interview. Complete the sentence. — 2

   It is crucial to find out about _____ and

   you have to know exactly _____ .

(f) Why should you not worry if you do not get the job? Give details. — 1

[Turn over

Text 3

You read an article about high street travel agencies.

Las nuevas agencias de viajes

Ya se sabe que las agencias de viajes, estas tiendas donde se puede reservar las vacaciones, han sufrido económicamente estos años. La crisis económica, la compra directa por Internet de billetes de avión, o la compra de noches de hotel desde el móvil han provocado una destrucción de las agencias de viajes.

Según un estudio recién publicado, el 66% de los viajes internacionales en el mundo ya se reservan desde Internet. Pero no todo está perdido para las agencias y el futuro parece un poco más positivo: existen nuevos negocios para el turismo de solteros o las visitas a balnearios.

Javier Mieres, propietario de *Endeavor*, una agencia especializada en organizar vacaciones fuera de lo normal, dice que "la gente se cansa de la playa y quiere algo que acorde con sus aficiones". Su agencia se creó hace seis años, en la crisis, y ha tenido un gran éxito. Javier pone como ejemplos que sus ingresos este año han aumentado y que va a abrir una sucursal nueva el mes que viene. Según Javier, hace falta que las agencias de viajes hagan lo siguiente para sobrevivir: ofrecer algo diferente y anticipar los deseos de los clientes.

Questions

(a) According to the article, travel agencies have suffered losses in recent years. What reasons does the article give for this? State any **two**. **2**

(b) The future seems more positive for travel agencies. What new business is there? State **two** things. **2**

(c) Javier Mieres owns a travel agency.

   (i) What does his agency specialise in? **1**

   (ii) What does he say about people's holiday habits? Complete the sentence. **2**

     People are _____ and they want

     a holiday that _____ .

   (iii) Javier's travel agency has been very successful. What examples does he give of this? State any **one**. **1**

   (iv) According to Javier, what do travel agencies have to do to survive? State **two** things. **2**

[END OF QUESTION PAPER]

ADDITIONAL SPACE FOR ANSWERS

FOR OFFICIAL USE

N5 National Qualifications 2017

Mark

X769/75/02

Spanish Writing

WEDNESDAY, 3 MAY
1:00 PM – 2:30 PM

Fill in these boxes and read what is printed below.

Full name of centre

Town

Forename(s)

Surname

Number of seat

Date of birth
Day Month Year

Scottish candidate number

Total marks — 20

Write your answer clearly, in **Spanish**, in the space provided in this booklet.

You may use a Spanish dictionary.

Additional space for answers is provided at the end of this booklet.

Use **blue** or **black** ink.

There is a separate question and answer booklet for Reading. You must complete your answers for Reading in the question and answer booklet for Reading.

Before leaving the examination room you must give both booklets to the Invigilator; if you do not, you may lose all the marks for this paper.

SQA

Total marks — 20

You are preparing an application for the job advertised below and you write an e-mail in **Spanish** to the company.

Se requiere camarero/camarera

Buscamos camarero/camarera para trabajar en el *Hotel Girasol* en Ibiza durante los meses de julio y agosto.

Se necesita experiencia previa y hay que hablar español e inglés.

Los interesados deben mandar un email a girasol@hotelesespanoles.com

---

To help you to write your e-mail, you have been given the following checklist.

You must include **all** of these points:

- Personal details (name, age, where you live)
- School/college/education experience until now
- Skills/interests you have which make you right for the job
- Related work experience
- Your level of Spanish
- Why you want this job

Use all of the above to help you write the e-mail in **Spanish**. The e-mail should be approximately 120–150 words. You may use a Spanish dictionary.

ANSWER SPACE

ANSWER SPACE (continued)

ANSWER SPACE (continued)

ANSWER SPACE (continued)

[END OF QUESTION PAPER]

ADDITIONAL SPACE FOR ANSWERS

ADDITIONAL SPACE FOR ANSWERS

FOR OFFICIAL USE

N5 National Qualifications 2017

Mark

X769/75/03

Spanish Listening

WEDNESDAY, 3 MAY
2:50 PM – 3:20 PM (approx)

Fill in these boxes and read what is printed below.

Full name of centre

Town

Forename(s)

Surname

Number of seat

Date of birth
Day   Month   Year

Scottish candidate number

Total marks — 20

Attempt ALL questions.

You will hear two items in Spanish. **Before you hear each item, you will have one minute to study the questions.** You will hear each item three times, with an interval of one minute between playings. You will then have time to answer the questions before hearing the next item.

You may NOT use a Spanish dictionary.

Write your answers clearly, in **English**, in the spaces provided in this booklet. Additional space for answers is provided at the end of this booklet. If you use this space you must clearly identify the question number you are attempting.

Use **blue** or **black** ink.

You are not allowed to leave the examination room until the end of the test.

Before leaving the examination room you must give this booklet to the Invigilator; if you do not, you may lose all the marks for this paper.

SQA

Total marks — 20

Attempt ALL questions

Item 1

Ana talks about technology.

(a) Where does Ana live? State any **one** thing. — 1

(b) Ana mentions the advantages of having a mobile phone. Complete the sentences. — 2

Thanks to my mobile, I can _____.

Also, it allows me to _____ on the school bus in the morning.

(c) Ana's parents didn't allow her to have a mobile phone when she was younger. How did she spend her free time? State **two** things. — 2

(d) When did she get a tablet computer? State any **one** thing. — 1

(e) Apart from technology, what other interests does she have? State **two** things. — 2

Item 2

Ana talks to Javi about television.

(a) How much time does Ana spend watching television per day? **1**

_____

(b) What does she say about the amount of television she watches? Tick (✓) the correct statement. **1**

	Tick (✓)
She does not think she watches too much television.	
She would like to be able to watch more television.	
She watches as much television as she can.	

(c) When does Ana watch television? State any **one** thing. **1**

_____

(d) Why does she never watch television before she goes to school in the morning? State any **two** things. **2**

_____

_____

(e) Why does she like music programmes? State any **one** thing. **1**

_____

(f) (i) Why does she not like soap operas? State any **one** reason. **1**

_____

(ii) What would she like to see more of? State any **one** thing. **1**

_____

_____

[Turn over for next question

Item 2 (continued)

(g) Ana almost never watches television with her family.

   (i) Why is this? Give **two** reasons. 2

   (ii) What does she do instead with her family? State **two** things. 2

[END OF QUESTION PAPER]

ADDITIONAL SPACE FOR ANSWERS

ADDITIONAL SPACE FOR ANSWERS

N5 National Qualifications 2017

X769/75/13

Spanish
Listening Transcript

WEDNESDAY, 3 MAY

2:50 PM – 3:20 PM (approx)

This paper must not be seen by any candidate.

The material overleaf is provided for use in an emergency only (eg the recording or equipment proving faulty) or where permission has been given in advance by SQA for the material to be read to candidates with additional support needs. The material must be read exactly as printed.

Instructions to reader(s):

For each item, read the English **once**, then read the Spanish **three times**, with an interval of 1 minute between the three readings. On completion of the third reading, pause for the length of time indicated in brackets after the item, to allow the candidates to write their answers.

Where special arrangements have been agreed in advance to allow the reading of the material, those sections marked **(f)** should be read by a female speaker and those marked **(m)** by a male; those sections marked **(t)** should be read by the teacher.

(t) Item Number One

Ana talks about technology.

You now have one minute to study the questions for Item Number One.

(f) Yo uso bastante la tecnología y no hay duda de que tiene muchas ventajas para mí. Por ejemplo, vivo en un pueblo pequeño a unos treinta kilómetros de la ciudad. Entonces, gracias a mi móvil, puedo mantenerme en contacto con todos mis amigos. También, me permite escuchar música en el autobús escolar por la mañana.

Cuando era más joven, mis padres no me dejaban tener un móvil así que pasaba mi tiempo libre jugando en el jardín y cuando hacía mal tiempo, veía los dibujos animados.

Hace cinco años recibí una tablet como regalo de Navidad. A partir de ese momento, me interesé mucho más en la tecnología. Claro que es esencial que los jóvenes además tengan otros intereses. A mí me encanta leer revistas y tocar la guitarra en un grupo que he formado con unos amigos.

Pero, vamos, hay que reconocer que la tecnología tiene un papel muy importante en el mundo actual.

(2 minutes)

(t) **Item Number Two**

Ana talks to Javi about television.

You now have one minute to study the questions for Item Number Two.

(m) Bueno Ana, ¿te gusta mucho la tele?

(f) Sí, ¡me encanta la tele! En general, paso unas cuatro horas al día viéndola.

(m) Eso es mucho, ¿no?

(f) Pues, la verdad es que no me parece demasiado. Creo que es lo normal.

(m) ¿Cuándo ves la tele?

(f) Bueno . . . suelo ver la tele después de hacer mis deberes y a veces a la hora de cenar.

(m) Y tus padres, ¿qué dicen?

(f) ¡Mis padres piensan que soy adicta! Pero no es verdad. Por ejemplo, nunca veo la tele por la mañana antes de ir al instituto porque siempre me levanto tarde, tengo que hacer la cama y pasear al perro.

(m) ¿Y qué tipo de programas te gustan?

(f) Me interesan los programas de música porque son divertidos y me relajan.

(m) En cuanto a la tele, ¿hay cosas que no te gustan?

(f) Sí, no me gustan nada las telenovelas porque me parecen tontas y no son realistas. Por otra parte me interesaría ver más películas extranjeras y concursos de cocina.

(m) Y tú, Ana, ¿ves la tele con tu familia?

(f) No, casi nunca porque a mis padres y a mí, no nos gustan los mismos programas. Y mi hermano piensa que la tele es una pérdida de tiempo y prefiere salir con sus amigos.

(m) Entonces, ¿cómo pasas el tiempo con tu familia?

(f) Pues, comemos juntos y visitamos a la abuela cada fin de semana.

(2 minutes)

(t) **End of test.**

Now look over your answers.

[END OF TRANSCRIPT]

NATIONAL 5
Answers

# ANSWERS FOR SQA NATIONAL 5 SPANISH 2017

NATIONAL 5 SPANISH 2015

Reading

Text 1

(a) Want/wish/desire/need money
NB: Should have feeling of desire

(b) *Any one from:*
- Become/be independent
- Explore/see world of work/business
- Source of income

(c)
- Go out to party/go out in the town/binge with friends
- Driving lessons/licence/test **or** to learn to drive

(d) *Any two from:*
- Stacking shelves in a supermarket
- Delivering papers/paper round
- Looking after/babysitting relatives' children

(e) *Any one from:*
- Teaches/helps her grandfather how to use the internet/go online
- Walks her neighbour's dogs

(f) (i) It's difficult to get up early/in the morning/for school

(ii) *Any one from:*
- Go to school/class tired/sleepy/fall asleep in class
- Don't have time for/skip breakfast
- Learn hardly anything/learn nothing

(g) **MIDDLE BOX** — Having a part-time job while studying is difficult for many young people
NB: If more than one box is ticked, 0 marks are awarded.

Text 2

(a) Fifth/5

(b)
- American sculptures
- Modern European art (in any order)

(c) They are going to love it/go crazy about it/go wild for it/be passionate about it/it will excite them

(d)
- Less well-known/less famous artists
- Of the last 50 years/50 years old/from 50 years ago

(e) (i) Voting for/choosing their favourite work of art/art/painting

(ii)
- Touch/interactive/tactile screens
- Survey/questionnaire/evaluation online/on the webpage

(f) Free days/open days/free access for retired people/pensioners/retired citizens/senior citizens

Text 3

(a)
- Fast/quickly/at excess speed
- Carelessly/without care/not sensibly/not wisely
NB: Accept responses in any order

(b) (To improve) safety

(c) *Any two from:*
- Facial expressions
- Muscle movements
- Emotions on the face

(d) *Any two from:*
- If the driver is distracted/absent minded/not concentrating
- If the driver is sleepy/drowsy/tired
- If the driver is not in a condition to drive
NB: The driver only needs to be mentioned once

(e)
- Sound/set off an alarm 5 times
- If s/he is sleeping/asleep

(f) *Any one from:*
- Avoids/prevents an accident
- Reduces risks (of human error)

Writing

Candidates will write a piece of extended writing in the modern language by addressing six bullet points. These bullet points will follow on from a job-related scenario. The bullet points will cover the four contexts of society, learning, employability and culture to allow candidates to use and adapt learned material. The first four bullet points will be the same each year and the last two will change to suit the scenario. Candidates need to address these "unpredictable bullet points" in detail to access the full range of marks.

Category	Mark	Content	Accuracy	Language resource — variety, range, structures
Very good	20	The job advert has been addressed in a full and balanced way. The candidate uses detailed language. The candidate addresses the advert completely and competently, **including information in response to both unpredictable bullet points.** A range of verbs/verb forms, tenses and constructions is used. Overall this comes over as a competent, well thought-out and serious application for the job.	The candidate handles all aspects of grammar and spelling accurately, although the language may contain one or two minor errors. Where the candidate attempts to use language more appropriate to Higher, a slightly higher number of inaccuracies need not detract from the overall very good impression.	The candidate is comfortable with the first person of the verb and generally uses a different verb in each sentence. Some modal verbs and infinitives may be used. There is good use of adjectives, adverbs and prepositional phrases and, where appropriate, word order. There may be a range of tenses. The candidate uses co-ordinating conjunctions and/or subordinate clauses where appropriate. The language of the e-mail flows well.
Good	16	The job advert has been addressed competently. There is less evidence of detailed language. The candidate uses a reasonable range of verbs/verb forms. Overall, the candidate has produced a genuine, reasonably accurate attempt at applying for the specific job, **even though he/she may not address one of the unpredictable bullet points.**	The candidate handles a range of verbs fairly accurately. There are some errors in spelling, adjective endings and, where relevant, case endings. Use of accents is less secure, where appropriate. Where the candidate is attempting to use more complex vocabulary and structures, these may be less successful, although basic structures are used accurately. There may be one or two examples of inaccurate dictionary use, especially in the unpredictable bullet points.	There may be repetition of verbs. There may be examples of listing, in particular when referring to school/college experience, without further amplification. There may be one or two examples of a co-ordinating conjunction, but most sentences are simple sentences. The candidate keeps to more basic vocabulary, particularly in response to either or both unpredictable bullet points.

Category	Mark	Content	Accuracy	Language resource — variety, range, structures
Satisfactory	12	The job advert has been addressed fairly competently. The candidate makes limited use of detailed language. The language is fairly repetitive and uses a limited range of verbs and fixed phrases, eg *I like, I go, I play*. The candidate copes fairly well with areas of personal details, education, skills, interests and work experience but does not deal fully with the two unpredictable bullet points **and indeed may not address either or both of the unpredictable bullet points.** On balance however the candidate has produced a satisfactory job application in the specific language.	The verbs are generally correct, but may be repetitive. There are quite a few errors in other parts of speech — gender of nouns, cases, singular/plural confusion, for instance. Prepositions may be missing, eg *I go the town*. Overall, there is more correct than incorrect.	The candidate copes with the first and third person of a few verbs, where appropriate. A limited range of verbs is used. Sentences are basic and mainly brief. There is minimal use of adjectives, probably mainly after *is* eg *Chemistry is interesting*. The candidate has a weak knowledge of plurals. There may be several spelling errors, eg reversal of vowel combinations.
Unsatisfactory	8	The job advert has been addressed in an uneven manner and/or with insufficient use of detailed language. The language is repetitive, eg *I like, I go, I play* may feature several times. There may be little difference between Satisfactory and Unsatisfactory. **Either or both of the unpredictable bullet points may not have been addressed.** There may be one sentence which is not intelligible to a sympathetic native speaker.	Ability to form tenses is inconsistent. There are errors in many other parts of speech — gender of nouns, cases, singular/plural confusion, for instance. Several errors are serious, perhaps showing mother tongue interference. The detail in the unpredictable bullet points may be very weak. Overall, there is more incorrect than correct.	The candidate copes mainly only with the personal language required in bullet points 1 and 2. The verbs "is" and "study" may also be used correctly. Sentences are basic. An English word may appear in the writing. There may be an example of serious dictionary misuse.

Category	Mark	Content	Accuracy	Language resource – variety, range, structures
Poor	4	The candidate has had considerable difficulty in addressing the job advert. There is little evidence of the use of detailed language. Three or four sentences may not be understood by a sympathetic native speaker. **Either or both of the unpredictable bullet points may not have been addressed.**	Many of the verbs are incorrect. There are many errors in other parts of speech – personal pronouns, gender of nouns, cases, singular/plural confusion, prepositions, for instance. The language is probably inaccurate throughout the writing.	The candidate cannot cope with more than one or two basic verbs. The candidate displays almost no knowledge of the present tense of verbs. Verbs used more than once may be written differently on each occasion. Sentences are very short. The candidate has a very limited vocabulary. Several English words may appear in the writing. There are examples of serious dictionary misuse.
Very poor	0	The candidate is unable to address the job advert. **The two unpredictable bullet points may not have been addressed.** Very little is intelligible to a sympathetic native speaker.	Virtually nothing is correct.	The candidate may only cope with the verbs *to have* and *to be*. Very few words are written correctly in the modern language. English words are used. There may be several examples of mother tongue interference. There may be several examples of serious dictionary misuse.

Listening

Item 1

(a) *Any one from:*
   - Swiss/from Switzerland
   - Speaks/knows/understands many/lots of languages
   - Speaks French, Italian and German **(any 2 languages)**

(b) *Any one from:*
   - She has an enthusiastic teacher
   - (Learns/sings) songs
   - Teacher has good sense of humour
   NB: Ignore gender

(c) Interactive board/Smart board/active board/interactive screens/touch screens

(d) She helps/talks to/speaks to/communicates with tourists (visiting her town)

(e) Ireland
   NB: Ignore wrong compass point

(f)
   - Work for an international company/business/firm/office
   - Travel/see/go around the world

(g) **BOTTOM BOX** — they play an important part in many areas of her life
   NB: If more than one box is ticked, 0 marks are awarded.

Item 2

(a) Three hours
   NB: Ignore additional information

(b)
   - **BOX 2** — the first exam is Biology
   - **BOX 4** — they last for 17 days in total
   NB: If three boxes ticked, maximum 1 mark; if four boxes ticked, 0 marks are awarded.

(c) *Any two from:*
   - It's not easy working alone
   - Learns better/more
   - Time passes quicker/quickly/fast/faster
   - Not so bored/not boring

(d) *Any two from:*
   - Eats biscuits
   - Calls/phones/talks/speaks to/chats with friends
   - Watches a soap opera/TV series/TV drama

(e) (Remembering/memorising/learning) the dates

(f) *Any two from:*
   - Be/go/relax outdoors/outside/in the open air/out in fresh air
   - Going out on his bike/cycling
   - Training with his swimming club/swimming

(g) *Any two from:*
   - It's on Wednesday
   - He hasn't worked (enough)/he hasn't done enough
   - He is not feeling well/feels ill/feels sick
   - He has a sore throat

NATIONAL 5 SPANISH 2016

Reading

Question			Expected Answer(s)	Max Mark
1.	(a)	(i)	over/more than 50 bags/bin bags	1
		(ii)	(around) 10am/10 in the morning	1
	(b)	(i)	damage (to the coast)	1
		(ii)	• cigarette butts/ends • broken/smashed/pieces of glass • supermarket bags (Any 2 from 3)	2
	(c)		protect/maintain the beauty of the beach(es)/keep the beach beautiful	1
	(d)		throwing/dropping waste/rubbish into the sea/ocean/water	1
	(e)	(i)	the environment interests them/they are interested in the environment	1
		(ii)	• park clean-ups/clear-up/tidy up the park *NB: ignore any mention of journey* • school visits/visits to school/going to school(s)	2
2.	(a)		lack/shortage of/don't get enough/not having an education	1
	(b)		• to recognise the (human) rights of girls • to address/solve/find a solution to the problems faced by girls/their problems • to increase the number/amount of girls who complete/get/have a (basic) education/schooling/school **(Any 2 from 3)**	2
	(c)		• do not complete secondary/high school (education) • illiterate *NB: blanks must be in the correct order*	2
	(d)		• the least/less well-paid/badly paid (jobs) • the least/less valued jobs/less value • domestic service/housekeeping/household chores/housework/house service/home service **(Any 2 from 3)**	2
	(e)		• study/go to school for 1 more year/a year longer/another year • a chance of/access to better jobs/employment/get better jobs • generate/earn/get <u>more</u> income/money for their families	3

Question			Expected Answer(s)	Max Mark
3.	(a)		• better/good/improved access to the Internet • communication technologies/ technology to communicate/ communicate through technology	2
	(b)	(i)	increases productivity/more productive/improves production *NB: ignore reference to employers/ employees*	1
		(ii)	balance work (life) with family/ personal (life)/work-life balance	1
	(c)		• she can be/stay in touch with/ communicate with/contact her colleagues/workmates/co-workers (online) • she can stay in touch/work/do this from home/café/park *NB: any 2 places needed*	2
	(d)		• she gets up/gets out of bed early • she eats/has breakfast • she reads/checks/looks at emails • she puts on/wears/picks comfortable clothes • she walks/goes to the living room/lounge **(Any 3 from 5)**	3
	(e)		**BOTTOM BOX** – Working from home has many advantages *NB: if more than one box is ticked, 0 marks are awarded*	1

Writing

Please see the assessment criteria for Writing on pages 102–104.

Listening

Question			Expected Answer(s)	Max Mark
1.	(a)		• in the morning/every morning/ when she gets up • an hour and a half/1 hour 30 mins	2
	(b)		grandfather/grandpa/papa/granda	1
	(c)		romance/romantic/love (novels/ stories/books)	1
	(d)		• a little/a bit/quite/slightly boring • not realistic/unrealistic **(Any 1 from 2)**	1
	(e)		• to download apps/applications • to shop/buy/shopping (online)/ buying things/stuff/internet shopping	2
	(f)		**BOX 2** – she reads for enjoyment *NB: if more than one box is ticked, 0 marks are awarded*	1
2.	(a)		two years/summers ago	1
	(b)		four days	1
	(c)		(she can see) different artists/ groups/bands/musicians/singers on the same day/throughout the day/ on the one day	1
	(d)		• cinema/films/movies • theatre/plays • competitions/contests • dance/dancing • exhibitions/shows **(Any 2 from 5)**	2
	(e)		• to have a rest/to relax/chill out • to meet/to get to know people from all over the world/from other countries	2
	(f)	(i)	her parents don't like it/camping	1
		(ii)	• in her uncle's house/home/with her uncle/at her uncle's • in a house in the centre of the town/village • in a house in a nearby town/ village **(Any 1 from 3)**	1
	(g)		• she is older/old enough/grown up • they trust her • she is more independent/ independent enough **(Any 2 from 3)**	2
	(h)		**BOX 2** – enjoying the atmosphere *NB: if more than one box is ticked, 0 marks are awarded*	1

NATIONAL 5 SPANISH
2017

Reading

Text 1

(a) A <u>very</u> powerful tool

(b) • Free/cost nothing
  • Increase/improve pupil/student motivation

(c) • Development of/develops technology/IT/ICT
  • Promotes/shows/makes them aware of different uses of mobiles/phones

(d) • (Take/have) a break/a rest/time out/a pause from technology/IT/ICT/put technology on hold
  • To relate/talk/connect to classmates/companions in class face to face

(e) Everyone uses them/it in everyday/daily life

(f) • Turn/switch/put on the/your mobiles/phones
  • <u>Instead of/rather than</u> open the/your books

Text 2

(a) 16–25

(b) • A (university) degree/university qualification/diploma
  • <u>Several/various/a few/some years</u> of work experience

(c) • (Young) people for part-time jobs/work/contracts/hours
  • (People for) fixed-term/period/time contracts/people to hire/who can work for a fixed time
  NB "people" need only be mentioned once in the candidate's answer.

(d) (i) To fund/pay for/finance/cover his everyday/daily life/expenses
  (ii) <u>A selection of/a lot of/many</u> jobs/offers/job offers

(e) • The company's/firm's/business'/enterprise's values
  • What the job/work is about/involves/deals with

(f) You will/could/can find/get/have your dream job some/one/any day

Text 3

(a) *Any two from*:
  • The economic/financial crisis/recession
  • Buying/booking/shopping for airline/plane tickets/flights <u>online/on the internet</u>
  • Buying nights in a hotel/booking hotels <u>from a mobile/phone</u>

(b) • Tourism for single people/singles/people on their own/bachelors/single men/single tourists
  • Spas/health/seaside resorts
  NB single tourists who visit spas/seaside resorts = 1 mark

(c) (i) Out/outside of the ordinary/norm/unusual holidays/holidays that aren't normal
  (ii) • Tired/fed up/bored of the beach/seaside
    • Matches/in keeping/agrees/in harmony with their hobbies/interests/likes/likings

(iii) *Any one from*:
  • It was created/opened during the (economic) crisis/recession
  • Income has increased/better income
  • (He is) opening/opens a new/another branch/shop/office

(iv) • Offer/do/have something different/different holidays/things/deals
  • Anticipate/foresee/predict customers'/clients' wishes/desires/wants

Writing

Please see the assessment criteria for Writing on pages 102–104.

Listening

Item 1

(a) *Any one from*:
  • Small town/village
  • 30 km from the city/town

(b) • Keep/stay in touch/maintain contact with friends
  • Listen to music

(c) • Played/playing in the garden
  • Watched/watching cartoons/animated films

(d) *Any one from*:
  • Five years ago
  • Christmas

(e) • Reading magazines
  • Plays guitar
  OR
  • Is in a group/band with friends

Item 2

(a) 4 hours

(b) She does not think she watches too much television (Box 1)

(c) *Any one from*:
  • After homework
  • At dinner/tea time

(d) *Any two from*:
  • Gets up late
  • Has to make her bed
  • Has to walk her dog
  (has to make her bed and walk the dog = 2 marks)

(e) *Any one from*:
  • They are fun
  • They relax me/they are relaxing

(f) (i) *Any one from*:
  • They're stupid/silly
  • They're not realistic/unrealistic/not real
  (ii) *Any one from*:
  • Foreign films/foreign cinema/films from abroad/films from other countries
  • Cookery competitions/cookery game shows

(g) (i) *Any two from*:
  • Her parents don't like the same programmes/don't like what she watches
  • Her brother thinks it's a waste of time
  • Her brother prefers going out with friends
  (ii) • Eat/have lunch/dinner
  • Visit gran/go and see gran

Acknowledgements

Permission has been sought from all relevant copyright holders and Hodder Gibson is grateful for the use of the following:

Image © Stokkete/Shutterstock.com (2015 Reading page 2);
Image © zhu difeng/Shutterstock.com (2015 Reading page 4);
Image © Zurijeta/Shutterstock.com (2015 Reading page 6);
Image © Alexander Gordeyev/Shutterstock.com (2016 Reading page 2);
Image © De Visu/Shutterstock.com (2016 Reading page 4);
Image © fonzales/Shutterstock.com (2016 Reading page 6);
Image © racorn/Shutterstock.com (2017 Reading page 2);
Image © gpointstudio/Shutterstock.com (2017 Reading page 4);
Image © Maksym Yemelyanov/stock.adobe.com (2017 Reading page 6).